Fighting for History

PIONEER EDITION

By Peter Winkler

CONTENTS

Across America, some people study the Fighting

Civil War in a special way. They relive it.

History

★ By Peter Winkler ★

Lots of people gathered at Cedar Creek. Tents stood in neat lines. Pots hung over campfires. Soldiers held their guns. A battle was near. Yet no one would get hurt.

These soldiers were **reenactors.** Those are people who act out past events. They were acting out a Civil War battle. It took place in 1864. It is called the Battle of Cedar Creek.

For the reenactors, the battle felt real. They smelled the smoke from guns. They felt what it was like to be in battle.

A House Divided

In the Civil War, Americans fought one another. The war tore the country apart. How could that happen?

In the 1800s, some Americans had slaves. A slave is a person owned by another person. But not everyone agreed with **slavery.** People had different ideas about it.

In the South, people wanted slavery. Slaves helped them farm their land. In the North, people were against slavery. They thought it should not be allowed.

☆ Divided States ☆

Disagreements about slavery tore America apart during the 1860s. Union states (blue) remained loyal to the United States. Confederate states (gray) broke away to form a new country. Territories (tan) did not belong to any state at the time.

OREG.

MINN.

N.H.

VT.

ME.

WIS.

MICH.

N.Y.

MASS.

R.I.

U.S. TERRITORIES

IOWA

OHIO

PA.

CONN.

N.J.

ILL.

IND.

DEL.

CALIF.

KANS.

MO.

W. VA.

VA.

MD.

KY.

N.C.

TENN.

ARK.

S.C.

MISS.

ALA.

GA.

TEX.

LA.

FLA.

N
W   E
S

☐ UNION STATES
☐ CONFEDERATE STATES
☐ TERRITORIES

WALTER P. CALAHAN (PHOTOS); NG MAPS

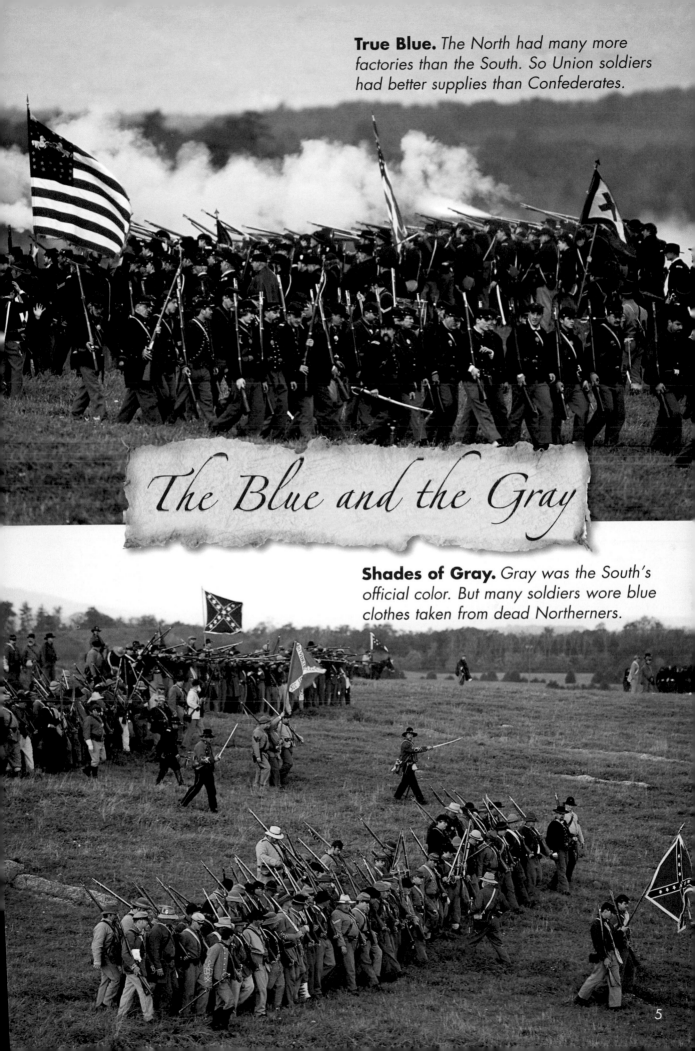

True Blue. *The North had many more factories than the South. So Union soldiers had better supplies than Confederates.*

The Blue and the Gray

Shades of Gray. *Gray was the South's official color. But many soldiers wore blue clothes taken from dead Northerners.*

An Uncivil War

The North and South disagreed. Still, they stayed together. But then Abraham Lincoln became President.

Lincoln wanted to end slavery. The South was afraid. So southern states **seceded,** or broke away. They were known as **Confederate** states.

President Lincoln would not let the country split apart. So he sent soldiers to take back the South. The soldiers were from the **Union,** or United States.

The Civil War began in 1861. It lasted four years.

Small Battle, Big Ending

In 1864, Union troops marched into Virginia. They tried to cut off the food supply. This would make it hard for southern troops.

In October, the two sides met at Cedar Creek. The battle was close. It looked like the South might win. But the Union troops held on. The North won the battle.

The Battle of Cedar Creek helped to end the war. Six months later, the South gave up. They became part of the United States again.

Getting It Right

The battle happened more than 140 years ago. In 2004, people acted it out. The reenactors worked hard. They wanted to get everything right.

Brian Barron was one of them. He had to learn how Civil War drummers held their sticks. It was a small detail. But it was important. So he learned to play his drum the old-fashioned way.

The Power of the Past

The reenactors at Cedar Creek made history come to life. They felt what it was like to be in the Civil War.

"You think about folks dying on this same ground," said Lew Ulrich. "One guy sat in his tent crying. That is how much it affects you." History can do that.

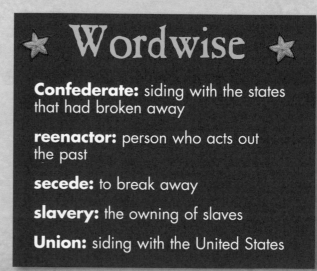

★ Wordwise ★

Confederate: siding with the states that had broken away

reenactor: person who acts out the past

secede: to break away

slavery: the owning of slaves

Union: siding with the United States

Drummer Boy. *"It's fun to be out here," said Confederate reenactor Max Glazier. Thousands of boys served as Civil War drummers. Drumbeats helped soldiers march properly.*

AMARIA STENZEL (USS CONSTITUTION); BATES LITTLEHALES (COINS).

History

Reenactors can bring the past to life. But you can too. Just visit a historical park.

There are many of them in the United States. Each lets you step back in time. You can feel what our country was like in the past.

Let's explore four of these parks. Take a close look at them. Where are they? How do they bring history to life?

The Freedom Trail

Have you ever heard of the Freedom Trail? It is a red line. It is painted on sidewalks in Boston, Massachusetts. It takes you on a walk through history.

Along the way, you can see actors. They pretend to live in the 1700s. Some are "planning" the Boston Tea Party. You can also board the U.S.S. *Constitution*. Learn why this ship became famous in 1812.

All Aboard. *Visitors travel back in time on board the U.S.S. Constitution in Boston (left) and a canal boat in Washington, D.C. (right).*

Brought to Life

The C&O Canal

The Chesapeake & Ohio Canal is another historical park. It is 184 miles long! It runs from Washington, D.C., to Cumberland, Maryland.

The canal was like a road made of water. Long ago, people used it for shipping. Boats traveled along the canal. They carried coal and other goods. They moved food and building supplies.

On the Water

Canal boats did not have motors. They were pulled by mules. The mules walked on dirt trails beside the canal. They pulled the boats with ropes.

Today, the boats still run. But they no longer carry goods. They carry visitors. In Washington, D.C., you can catch a ride. A guide tells stories about the history of the canal.

Climbing Into the Past.
Visitors can explore ancient cliffside homes at Bandelier National Monument.

Bandelier National Monument

The Bandelier National Monument is in New Mexico. It honors Native American history.

Ancient Pueblo lived here long ago. They made their homes in the the canyons. Today, you can visit these homes. Some are in caves. Others sit on the tops of cliffs. These homes tell us about the lives of the ancient Pueblo.

Exploring the Past

To visit, pull on your hiking boots. Then walk along the trail. It winds past old Pueblo homes. Climb up wooden ladders and look inside. See where people lived hundreds of years ago.

Later, you can make crafts with local Native Americans. You can also take a walk at night. A ranger will lead you through the park.

A Dark History. *At the Alcatraz prison, people tour cells that once held dangerous criminals.*

Alcatraz Island

Historical parks also show the recent past. That is true at Alcatraz. This island is in California. It is home to a famous prison. It held some of country's worst criminals.

Today, no one lives at the prison. It closed in 1963. But you can visit it. Take a tour with a park ranger. Find out what it was like to live and work inside the prison.

More History to Explore

There are many ways to learn about history. You can read a book. You can watch a film. But if you want to feel the past, head for a historical park.

Across the country, these parks give you a special view into the past. They let you discover history in all sorts of places. At historical parks, you do not just read about history. You live it.

Living History

Take a shot at these questions to find out what you learned from the book.

1 Why did Americans fight the Civil War?

2 Why was the Battle of Cedar Creek important?

3 How do reenactors bring history to life?

4 How is visiting a historical park different from reading a book?

5 Which park would you most like to visit? Why?